In honor of

Phyllis Baker Vandewater
and
Emily Robinson Vandewater

Great African Americans

Ida B. Wells-Barnett

a voice against violence

Revised Edition

Patricia and Fredrick McKissack

Series Consultant
Dr. Russell L. Adams, Chairman
Department of Afro-American Studies, Howard University

Enslow Publishers, Inc.

40 Industrial Road	PO Box 38
Box 398	Aldershot
Berkeley Heights, NJ 07922	Hants GU12 6BP
USA	UK

http://www.enslow.com

For Ann and Jerome Hamilton

Revised edition of *Ida B. Wells-Barnett: A Voice Against Violence* © 1991

Library of Congress Cataloging-in-Publication Data

McKissack, Pat, 1944-
Ida B. Wells-Barnett : a voice against violence / Patricia McKissack
and Fredrick McKissack.—Rev. ed.
     p. cm. — (Great African Americans series)
Includes index.
  ISBN 0-7660-1677-3
1. Wells-Barnett, Ida B., 1862-1931—Juvenile literature. 2. Afro-American women
civil rights workers—Biography—Juvenile literature. 3. Civil rights workers—United States—
Biography—Juvenile literature. 4. Journalists—United States—Biography—Juvenile literature.
5. Afro-Americans—Social conditions—Juvenile literature. 6. Lynching—United States—
History—Juvenile literature. 7. United States—Race relations—Juvenile literature.
[1. Wells-Barnett, Ida B., 1862-1931. 2. Civil rights workers. 3. Journalists. 4. Afro-Americans—
Biography. 5. Women—Biography.] I. McKissack, Fredrick. II. Title.
E185.97.W55 M37   2001
973.04'96073'0092—dc21   00-009422

Printed in the United States of America

10 9 8 7 6 5 4 3 2

To Our Readers: We have done our best to make sure all Internet addresses in this book were active and appropriate when we went to press. However, the author and the publisher have no control over and assume no liability for the material available on those Internet sites or on other Web sites they may link to. Any comments or suggestions can be sent by e-mail to comments@enslow.com or to the address on the back cover.

Every effort has been made to locate all copyright holders of material used in this book.
If any errors or omissions have occurred, corrections will be made in future editions of this book.

Illustration Credits: Department of Special Collections, University of Chicago Library, pp. 4, 14, 18, 19, 21, 24, 27, 29; Dover Publications, Inc., p. 16; Library of Congress, pp. 20, 23, 25; Marshall County Historical Museum, Holly Springs, Mississippi, pp. 6, 7, 9; National Archives, p.15; Schomburg Center for Research in Black Culture, New York Public Library, pp. 3, 13; Tennessee State Library and Archives Manuscript Division, p. 11; United States Postal Service, p. 26.

Cover Credits: Library of Congress; Department of Special Collections, University of Chicago; Schomburg Center for Research in Black Culture, New York Public Library.

TABLE of CONTENTS

ida B. Wells-Barnett
July 16, 1862–March 25, 1931

CHAPTER 1

Fever!

The Civil War ended in 1865, and so did slavery in America. Jim and Lizzie Wells were freed. So was their three-year-old daughter, Ida. The family lived in Holly Springs, Mississippi. Seven more children were born.

Ida was sent to school. Learning was easy for her. She liked to read, but writing was more fun. She made her parents proud. Besides being smart, Ida Wells grew into a pretty girl with honey-brown skin. She was also loving and kind.

This picture was taken in Holly Springs, Mississippi, around the same time that young Ida B. Wells lived there.

Then came the fever! Yellow fever was a killer disease. There was no cure at that time. Many good people died in Holly Springs. Jim and Lizzie were among them. So was their baby son.

Ida was just sixteen years old. Their Holly Springs neighbors wanted to take the children to live with them. But Ida kept her family together. They lived in the house her parents left for them. She got a job as a country school teacher to earn money.

The next year, Ida let other family members take the children. Ida moved to Memphis, Tennessee, and got another job teaching there.

6

Many people left Holly Springs in 1858 because they did not want to become sick with yellow fever.

CHAPTER 2

First Fight for Freedom

a fter the Civil War, laws were passed that protected the rights of all Americans regardless of color. Blacks had the same rights as whites. They rode in train cars together, sat together in public places, and shared the same public drinking fountains. But by 1878, laws began to change.

Ida taught in a one-room, country school just outside Memphis. She rode the train into town at the end of each week.

After the Civil War, new schools were started because the freed slaves did not know how to read and write. This is one of the first schools for black children in Holly Springs.

One day Ida bought a train ticket to Memphis. She took a seat in the front car. The conductor said Ida had to move to the car where men who smoked rode. It was called a smoker car.

Why? She was black. For many years, it was against the law to make people sit in separate cars because of their color. Ida did not know that this law had changed. She would not move. The conductor took her arm. She bit him. He called for help. Another man came. They picked Ida up and made her move. No one helped her.

Ida would not sit in the smoker car. Instead she got off the train.

Ida was very angry. She was twenty-one years old, and she decided to fight for her rights another way. She would take the railroad company to court. She found a lawyer to take her case. Months passed. Nothing happened. Ida learned that her lawyer had been paid off by the railroad company. She found another lawyer.

Finally, the case went to court. Ida won her case. The judge ordered the railroad company to pay Ida $500. It was her first fight for freedom!

The railroad took the case to another court, and this time, Ida lost.

From 1880 to 1900, states passed more laws that took away black people's rights. Ida would always speak out against unfair laws.

This is one of the papers from Ida's lawsuit against the railroad company.

CHAPTER 3

Violence

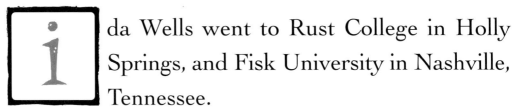da Wells went to Rust College in Holly Springs, and Fisk University in Nashville, Tennessee.

She still taught school in Memphis. Often Ida spoke out about how poor black schools were. She wrote for a church newspaper, *The Living Way*. She spoke up about rights and fair laws. Soon she was asked to write for other black newspapers, too.

In 1889, Ida became part owner of a Memphis newspaper, *Free Speech*. One day she wrote an article about the schools for black children in Memphis.

SOUTHERN HORRORS.

LYNCH LAW

IN ALL

ITS PHASES

Miss IDA B. WELLS,

Price, - - - Fifteen Cents.

THE NEW YORK AGE PRINT,

1892.

Ida wrote many articles and books to tell the world about lynching. She wanted more people to join her fight against this terrible crime. In 1892, the year she wrote *Southern Horrors*, 161 blacks were lynched in the United States.

She said they were run-down and crowded, and there were not enough books. Ida lost her teaching job after that. But she did not stop speaking out.

In many southern states, laws were being passed that took away the rights of African Americans. Some laws made it very hard for blacks to vote. When blacks tried to vote they were beaten. Their houses and businesses were burned. Many times they were hanged. Murdering people this way was called lynching.

Ida wrote about these terrible beatings, house burnings, and lynchings. She spoke out against the unfair laws that were being passed. Friends told her to be careful. Maybe she should stop. No! She would keep writing the stories.

Then, in the spring of 1892, three young black men were shot to death. They had done nothing wrong. Ida wanted people to protest this tragedy. "... Say or do something," Ida wrote. Very few people said or did anything.

Finally, a group of angry men burned the office of *Free Speech*. Ida got away just in time.

Frederick Douglass became famous for speaking out against slavery. Ida thought he was the greatest leader in American history.

Running wasn't easy for Ida. She wanted to stay in Memphis and fight against violence. Her friends said, go North. Go where it will be safe to speak out!

And so she did. Ida B. Wells went to New York. Her work was not over. It was really just beginning.

Ida moved to New York City in 1892. There she wrote many more articles against the evils of lynching.

CHAPTER 4

The Struggle Against Violence

da worked for the *New York Age* newspaper in New York. T. Thomas Fortune was the owner. He said Ida "had plenty of nerve." Those who knew Ida agreed with Mr. Fortune's words.

In 1893, Ida decided to move to Chicago. There she began writing for an African-American newspaper owned by Ferdinand L. Barnett. Ida went all over the United States and Europe asking people to join

Ida married
Ferdinand L.
Barnett, a
lawyer and
newspaper
owner. He
helped her
work against
lynching.

her in her fight. Thousands and thousands of people joined her.

In 1895, Ida wrote a small book named *A Red Record*. It showed that thousands of black men, women, and children had been lynched. Something had to be done to stop the violence against black people.

On June 27, 1895, Ida married Ferdinand L. Barnett. Many people wondered, would Ida give up her work? Not for long. When her first son, Charles, was six months old, Ida Wells-Barnett went back to work. With baby Charles at her side, she spoke all over the country. She even spoke to the president of the United States.

Ida with her first son, Charles, in 1896.

Ida was shocked and sickened to know that crowds of people liked to watch lynchings.

In 1898, Ida met with President William McKinley at the White House. She told him that ten thousand black men, women, and children had been lynched since the Civil War.

The president said he was shocked, but he did little to help. There was still violence. The fight against it went on, too. Ida Wells-Barnett made sure of that.

Ida with her four children in 1909: Charles, Herman, Ida, and Alfreda.

CHAPTER 5

No More Lynching!

Ida was not the only person speaking out against lynching. Other women joined her. They formed clubs called the Ida B. Wells Clubs. *No more lynching!* was their cry.

Women could not vote. Ida worked for women's rights, too. But it wasn't until 1920 that American women were given the right to vote.

She was also interested in children's rights. Ida pushed for better laws that protected children from violence, too.

In 1908, there was a race riot in Springfield,

**Ida believed that women should be allowed to vote.
In 1913, women from all over the United States marched in
Washington, D.C., to demand the right to vote.**

Ida and Ferdinand with their children and grandchildren.

Illinois. More killing . . . more burning. White and black Americans met in New York. Ida Wells-Barnett attended. Something had to be done about the lynchings, beatings, and burnings. Out of that meeting came the National Association for the Advancement of Colored People (NAACP). The

24

NAACP was formed in 1909 to help work for rights through the courts. The NAACP was also against the Ku Klux Klan (KKK), a hate group formed right after the Civil War.

For many years the KKK had not been very strong. But in 1915 the secret group started up

Ku Klux Klan members taught hatred to their children. They hid under white sheets as they spread violence and murder through the South.

again on Stone Mountain in Georgia. KKK members used violence and fear against people of color, Jews, and Catholics.

Ida Wells-Barnett worked all her life to stop the Ku Klux Klan. *No more lynching!* was her battle cry.

When the spring flowers bloomed in 1931, Ida B. Wells-Barnett got sick. Two days later, she died. Twenty years later, there was only one lynching reported in the United States. Ida's work had made a difference.

Top:
Ida's writing was her weapon against lynching. In the 1880s, many writers used typewriters like this.

Left:
In 1990, the U.S. Postal Service issued a stamp honoring Ida B. Wells.

Alfreda was proud to honor her mother's memory at a special event in 1963. With her is the Reverend Carl Fugua.

timeline

1862 —— Ida is born on July 16 in Holly Springs, Mississippi.

1878 —— Her parents die from yellow fever; Ida struggles to keep her family together.

1884 —— Wins a lawsuit against a railroad company.

1887 —— Railroad company takes the case to another court; this time Ida loses.

1888 —— Writes articles for newspapers.

1889 —— Becomes part owner of a newspaper in Memphis, Tennessee, *Free Speech*.

1909

1892 —— Uses her writing to fight against lynching; *Free Speech* offices are burned down; Ida moves to New York.

1896

1895 —— Marries Ferdinand L. Barnett on June 27.

1898 —— Meets President William McKinley to talk about lynching.

1909 —— Attends a meeting that leads to the founding of the National Association for the Advancement of Colored People (NAACP).

1930

1931 —— Dies on March 25.

WORDS TO KNOW

civil war—A war fought within one country. In the United States, the Civil War (1861–1865) was fought between northern and southern states.

disease—An illness or sickness.

Ku Klux Klan (KKK)—A race-hate group started after the Civil War.

The Living Way—A black church newspaper in Memphis, Tennessee, in the 1800s.

lynching—Illegal killing, usually by hanging; a murder done by a mob of people.

Free Speech—The newspaper Ida B. Wells-Barnett co-owned in Memphis, Tennessee.

National Association for the Advancement of Colored People (NAACP)—An organization started to help all Americans gain equal rights and protection under the law. The NAACP is one of the oldest civil rights organizations in the United States.

New York Age—A weekly black newspaper in New York in the late 1800s.

WORDS TO KNOW

president—The leader of a country or an organization.

race riot—Violence in the streets; violent acts against a race of people.

The Red Record—A book about lynchings, written by Ida B. Wells-Barnett in 1895.

slavery—The buying and selling of human beings.

smoker car—A train car for men who smoked. It was bad manners for men to smoke in front of women.

violence—Acts that hurt or destroy people, places, animals, and other things.

yellow fever—A disease that is carried by mosquitoes. It killed thousands of people in the late 1800s.

Learn More about Ida B. Wells-Barnett

Books

Fradin, Dennis and Judith B. Fradin. *Ida B. Wells: Mother of the Civil Rights Movement*. Boston, Mass.: Houghton Mifflin Company, 2000.

Freedman, Suzanne. *Ida B. Wells-Barnett & the Anti-Lynching Crusade*. Brookfield, Conn.: Millbrook Press, Inc., 1994.

Medearis, Angela S. *Princess of the Press: The Story of Ida B. Wells-Barnett*. New York: N. Y.: Penguin Putnam Books for Young Readers, 1997.

Welch, Catherine A. *Ida B. Wells-Barnett: Powerhouse with a Pen*. Minneapolis, Minn.: Lerner Publishing Group, 2000.

Internet Addresses

African American Perspectives, "The Progress of a People"
Part of the Library of Congress, this site has a brief biography of Ida B. Wells-Barnett.
<http://lcweb2.loc.gov/ammem/aap/idawells.html>

Just the Arti-Facts, "Ida B. Wells"
Just the Arti-Facts explores the life of this brave woman. Follow the links for more information.
<http://www.chicagohistory.org/AOTM/Mar98/mar98fact2.html>

index